MACKER

KITBAG FULL OF LIES

by

PADDY MCGOWAN and JAMES M HARPUR

Macker

Macker

also by

JAMES MICHAEL HARPUR

1798 DARK AND EVIL DAYS

BERGIN'S QUEST

BERGIN'S WAR

BLOOD LOTTERY

JOKES, TASTELESS, IRREVERENT AND FUNNY

MAN IN THE SHADOW

MAYGLASS CEILI BAND

SPENDER GENERAL

also by

JAMES MICHAEL HARPUR AND RICHARD DAVIS

WORLD WAR ONE LEGENDS AND MYTHS

Macker

Macker

ACKNOWLEDGMENTS

I owe a lot to this old sweat who would love to have written this book himself but I have taken up the mantle myself and related the stories to my good friend James Michael Harpur. He has collected a story I have written in longhand on foolscap pages each week at the Coolock Library Art class and typed it up on his computer. We did more talking than art. Thanks is also due to our editor Barry Vickers who made it all possible

Macker

2014

Macker

Macker

MACKER

KITBAG FULL OF LIES

Macker

Macker

Chapters

1. Private Mangan's Defence
2. Ten Mile Walk In Wicklow
9. Long Chase
4. Dub In Gorey
5. Turf Man
6. Gas Man
7. Compliment In Kind
8. Good News
9. Baptism Of Fire
10. Dead End Job
11. Dooley's Bicycle
12. Feed My Sheep
13. Sailors Beware
14. Poor Old Nag
15. At Face Value
16. Dublin Seanachai
17. Hungers Mother

Macker

18. Trenches
19. Duck the Bullets
20. One Sarge and his Dog
21. Enemy at the Gate
22. Think Tank
23. Two Places At Once
24. Big Bang Theory
25. Did You Hear What Your Man Said
26. Tuppence For All
27. By Special Delivery
28. Heinsie
29. Gift Horse
30. Big Stink
31. Pathfinder
32. Pathfinder 2
33. Wallpaper Party
34. Arm of Truth
35. Long Drop
36. Big Shine

Macker

37. I Spy With My Little Eye

38. That Dam Yank

39. Point Of Difference

40. Forehead

41. Noah Meets Columbus

42. Who Done It

43. News About News

44. Hearsay

45. Some Cat

46. Stamp of Approval

47. Things that go Bump in the Night

48. Ugg Lugg Maker

49. Bork Bork Story

50. Oh No Not You Again

Macker

Chapter 1

Private Mangan's Defence

My name is Patrick McGowan. Most people call me *"Macker"*. I am also known as the *"scrounger"*, a derogatory title but nevertheless in the army it was regarded as a highly respectable position. The role of this individual was mainly the acquisition of supplies for the troops with little or no questions asked.

However on this occasion I had been ordered to escort a Private Mangan from his place of incarceration to his place of judgement. He was facing a charge of being absent without leave, not having obtained the official permission. We marched

Macker

together from his cell and up into the office of the commanding officer. Other officials were present including a female officer who had crossed my path on more than one occasion. She had her notebook and sharpened pencil at the ready and relished the thought of the discomfort Mangan had to face. She was in fact the lady who had brought the charge against him in the first case.

Being A.W.O.L in the army was a serious misdemeanour, even in peace time, and the punishment could be very severe.

"You have been accused of being absent from your place of employment on Monday last, Private Mangan" said the commanding officer, reading from the charge sheet in front of him.

"Have you anything to say in your defence before I pass sentence".

I was waiting for him to don the dreaded black cap but this was me being melodramatic.

Macker

Young Private Mangan looked over at his accuser and standing to attention with his cap under his arm and his head held high shouted out in a loud voice.

"On the night in question the bitch had post natal depression which is the cause of my dereliction of duty, Sir"!

Before the commanding officer could ask any further questions he was interrupted by the female officer who was very irate.

"How dare you? How dare you degrade womanhood in such a demeaning manner, you dirty lout"?

Private Mangan replied in a calm voice.

"I'm not talking about the wife Ma'am. It's my dog. She had eleven pups on the night in question and in my concern for the poor animal I forgot to return to duty".

"Case dismissed".

I burst out laughing at the commanding officer's acquittal of Private Mangan .The face of the female officer dropped in amazement.

"Out, out! The lot of you" was the cry from our C.O. as we were ordered from the office. The red faced woman was ordered to stay back.

"I need to have a word with you lieutenant".

We roared with laughter all the way down the stairs. It was a victory but another nail in my coffin.

Macker

Chapter 2

Ten Mile Walk In Wicklow

"Right"!

The sergeant addressed the squad of soldiers standing to attention before him.

"Listen up you lot. At 0.600 hours tomorrow we start our ten mile hike in County Wicklow. Full combat gear and I want to see d'em back packs bulging. Do you hear-bulging. I want them so packed that I can't get a slide rule down the pack".

It was still dark the following morning when we embarked on our journey. Two army trucks carrying our squad pulled out of Mckee Barracks in the northern area of Dublin City and landed somewhere in Wicklow. It took me a while to get my

Macker

bearings. I had been in the county in my youth and had a fair idea of the layout of the land. We were near Baltyboys. So burdened down with bulging back packs our march started.

It was hilly terrain and with the weight of the back packs the troops found it hard going. We were gone about half way and the company rested for ten minutes. It was then that the Sarge became suspicious. Everyone around us were struggling with their backpacks. They must have weighted a ton. I actually thought that some of them had packed the kitchen sink (Belfast type-you might remember those old enamel monsters?) I already had my backpack on and it was then that the Sergeant copped on.

"McGowan front and centre! You're very fresh looking after our hard slog and showing no sign of fatigue. How can this be? We usually have to help each other to lift them off the ground".

Macker

He grabbed my backpack and found it was light as feather.

"Empty it now in front of all your comrades".

I pulled out two pillows.

"What's this McGowan"?

"Well Sarge, you told us to fill our sacks but you didn't say with what".

For my troubles I ended up carrying half of Wicklow the rest of the way home but I was learning my trade.

Macker

Macker

Chapter 3

Long Chase

Well me and my flatmates used to frequent Slattery's pub in Rathmines, it being close to Cathal Brugha Barracks in Dublin. We were generally there drinking on a regular basis. Being army it was expected of you. It was the local watering hole. I regarded one of my flatmates called Tom Lesley as a very shrewd fellow. If there were any flies on him you can bet they were paying rent.

Well there was this girl who put her eye on Tom. My God she had a face only a mother could love –pig ugly. When God was handing out good looks she wasn't in the queue. She pursued Tom everywhere he went. Poor Tom slipped out the backdoors of

Macker

more restaurants and bars than I can name to avoid her. On one occasion the poor man made his escape from Slattery's through a cellar door because the love of his life had came in through the back door to try and outwit Tom.

Two hours later Tom decided to return to the pub thinking that she would be gone. Slipping quietly into a large crowd in the Long Bench (so called because it was like a church bench) Tom squeezed himself to the very end of the wooden seat where I was sitting. He asked me to get us a couple of pints. While I was at the bar getting the drinks I noticed his women had found him again and they were sitting together deep in conversation. Suddenly she stood up and walked out.

I put the pints down in front of Tom wondering about the sudden departure of the woman and asked him the question uppermost in my mind.

"What on earth did you say to her, Tom"!

Macker

"I told her I was a body washer in the morgue".

"Good riddens" I said to Tom.

"Drink up-you had a lucky escape".

Macker

Macker

Chapter 4

Dub in Gorey

While I was serving in the Irish army I would often visit my Nan. I would travel every Saturday morning when I was off duty and do odd jobs around her house or just visit and chat with her. Well for weeks she was working on an Arran sweater. She was always knitting or crocheting for someone. The one she was working on this day was lilac in colour. Who in their right mind would wear such a thing? Well I was dumbfounded that Saturday when she said she had knitted it for me.

Macker

"Right she said take off that jacket and jumper and try it on. Let's see how it fits?"

It was a good fit.

"Look in the mirror".

"Wow"!

She had put the letter *"P"* on the right side of the jumper in white and it stood out like a sore thumb. I was in a way, proud to wear it, and on the other hand felt stupid. It made me look like a ponce. Ah well! I suppose she put a lot of work into it.

"Ho! By the way you're heading for the country this weekend".

"Yes Nan. My flat mates Fred and Tom have invited me down to Gorey".

In the mean time I picked up a nickname *"ET"* from the Stephen Spielberg film of the same name which was showing in town. I said my goodbyes to Nan and left for Gorey. When I arrived I was met by Fred's brother Pedro. We got squared away and we headed for Big Tom's pub.

Macker

"*I hope you brought your darts, ET,* said Pedro.

"*Yes your name has preceded you*".

So a few hours later and pints as well, myself and Pedro were doing well on the dart board and taking in a few bob as well. Suddenly I was getting funny looks from the locals. They seemed to be taking a great interest in my newly acquired sweater. At the same time I spotted Fred and Tom in the crowd. There were more and more people there and all looking at my sweater. Then a voice from the crowd roared out.

"Hay ET! What does the P on your pink jumper stand for, Ha Ha"?

"*Hang on minute lads, till I finish this game of darts*".

I needed a double two. Standing on the Oche my first dart went near and as did the second, but the third dart went in.

"*Right lads, you want to know what the P stands for? It does not stand for ET. It does not stand for Paddy, Its stands for...*".

Macker

I had their undivided attention.

"Pullover!"

The pub erupted into laughter and I knew I was an adopted Gorey man.

Macker

Chapter 5

Turf Man

Well, he was known by many names but army people generally referred to him as the *"Turf Man"*. The story goes that when he was a young buck corporal, he was put in charge of keeping the home fires burning. Yes-he was in charge of all the piles of turf in the barracks and implementation of supplies to that effect.

Months went by and soon he caught the eye of the P.A.S (Military Police). Yes-they took quiet an interest in our turf man. Soon after that he was arrested for stealing the turf and selling it to the local natives. He was convicted in an army court and sent to the *"digger"* (prison) for a month and loss of pay. His loss of pay helped to pay for the loss of

Macker

turf. When his time was up he was sent back to work on the barracks but not with turf on the orders of his superiors.

"By the way I'm curious" said the commanding officer.

"How long were you taking the turf and why? The money was it?"

"Well, Sir, it's like this. Can I be charged for the same crime twice"?

"I suppose not".

"Sir it was not the turf I was after. It was all them lovely wheelbarrows Sir, all twelve of them and Sir it was well worth a month in the digger".

Macker

Chapter 6

Gas Man

"McGowan"!

"You're wanted across the square in the C.O's office".

"Now"!

"What did I do"?

"Don't know - must be something bad. On the double...".

So I ran around the square. The square was sacred ground. I got to the C.O's office to be met by an officer who jobbed me a week earlier.

"What's it's about Sir"?

Macker

"You're a witness against Terrill the turf man".

"What has he done now"?

"Sorry, can't help you there because I'm up as well".

"You- Sir"?

"What in hell is going on"?

I was marched before the C.O. and went up to his desk, cap in hand.

"Well private in your own words. We would like to know what happened one week ago this day. By the way you're not on trial here today. So relax and take your time".

"Well Sir I was approached by the orderly officer of the day who wanted me to strip a house bare".

"Was this the vacant married officers' quarters"?

"O yes Sir".

"And what was your particular job"?

Macker

"Well sir my job was to disconnect all the domestic appliances in the house up and down stairs".

"What do you mean when you use the word domestic appliance"?

"Well Sir-wash hand basins, kitchen sink and cooker".

"You mean the gas cooker"?

"Is that why I'm here Sir"?

"As I have said before you are not on trial here private".

"Were you given any help on your endeavours private? After all it was some undertaking."

"O Yes Sir, a Corporal Tirrell assisted me".

"What was his job"?

"When I disconnected the appliance the corporal would dispose of the said item".

"Now private did you hear any orders being given to the said corporal that day"?

Macker

"Yes Sir. He was told not to leave anything behind. Strip bare everything nothing but the four wall s to be left stranding".

"What time did you finish your job private"?

"Five O Clock, Sir"?

"So you didn't see a delivery made to the house".

"No Sir".

"Sir! May I ask what's wrong"?

"Well your helper helped himself to that delivery after you left which was a six ring cooker".

"He did take his orders very seriously even to the letter sir".

So the *"turf man"* became the *"gas man"*.

Macker

Chapter 7

Compliment In Kind

I woke to the chatter of some good for nothing. There is always someone, the kind of guy who is always looking for attention.

"What day is it?"

"Monday".

"Rise and shine! Hand off jocks and on socks! Move it"!

This is bloody well like the song goes - *'I don't like Mondays'.* My tongue felt like the tongue of an old boot. I wish I could put my head in a vice grips. After breakfast, "y*acks*", we went out and paraded. *'Area'* (means attention) and we followed the drill. Quartermaster Butler took the parade. Why I don't know? Maybe the sergeant was sick?

Macker

"Right, lads! Look lively. Pauline is taking the parade".

She went through us like a snake full of venom. If looks could kill we were all dead.

"What is this Quartermaster? How dare you present your men in this deplorable state"?

"Sorry Ma'am the men were celebrating yesterday after their win".

"I don't care"!

"As usual Ma'am your wisdom prevails. If you were in India you would be sacred".

I took to a sudden bolt of laughter.

"McGowan, do not interrupt when the good quartermaster is passing me a compliment".

Of course she would never understand, would she?

I smiled to myself knowing the most sacred thing in India was a cow.

Macker

Chapter 8

Good News

"Well-Macker"!

"Today's the day"!

"I know. You're up before 'Big Foot' Pauline".

"Don't remind me Mango".

"What excuse do you have this time to get off the hook"?

"Would you believe, not a one"!

"Macker, she'll have a field day"!

"If I go down"?

"Ah well, Wardy is taking it- I think he'll go easy on me".

Macker

Later on I wait outside the Commanders office.

"Right in you go. Clea go sea. Deas go shea, ortaig"!

Mango came with me and I stood in front of the commanding officer.

"You are charged with being absent on Monday last contrary to the Act of 1954. Have you anything to say in your own defence before I pass sentence on you"?

Out of the corner eye I saw Pauline getting to her feet. Then it hit me.

"Well Sir! The day in question I got up about 10.30am. I went down to the local shop to get the 'Sunday Indo'. On picking up the paper I discovered it was Monday".

Mango burst into a loud laugh. The C.O. *'Wardy'* put his head in his hand and had a good laugh.

"Out the pair of you, case explained".

Macker

I believe my excuse was up for six weeks on the board of excuses and drove my Adjutant, Pauline mad.

When she had stood up in court she had revealed the "*Sunday indo*" on the chair under her.

Macker

Macker

Chapter 9

Baptism of fire

"Hey"!

"Are you, the new fellow- the welder"?

"I am"!

"The C.O. wants to see you! You will find him in the locker room".

I made my way as directed.

"Sir- Private McGowan! Sir"!

"Ah, Hah- the welder".

"Do you know how long we have been waiting for a welder"?

"Years"!

Macker

"Come, I want you to gaze at this table and tell me what you think of it".

"Well Sir, it's a tennis table Sir".

"Brilliant deduction on your part –private, but what is wrong with it"?

"Ooh, I see what you mean sir: it's barely supported by those two bedside lockers".

"Yes private and I want you to do something about it, this Friday weekend".

"Sir, yes Sir"

"...and drop the Sir. You'll find we are a bit more relaxed in this unit".

"So! McGowan, is it? By Friday"!

"Sir"!

I went to find a C.Q. (Quartermaster) who showed me the way to the store which was part of three workshops.

"What can I do you for, before you do it to me?" asked the Sergeant in charge.

Macker

"Well I'm looking for inch box tube-about ten lengths".

"Well fill in those three invoices"!

"Why three" I asked?

"That's the army way".

"Who am I to argue with a Sergeant"?

Well I finished all three forms.

The Sergeant examined them and looked up at me.

"Ah! I'm not sure we have that in stock, just let me check".

He went away to the back of the store room. About five minutes later he returned with a list.

"You look at that and tell me if what you are looking for is on that list".

I went up and down the list about four or five times.

"Yes Sergeant" I said.

Macker

The sergeant replied *"Good"*.

"But according to your list Sergeant, you have 1 inch and ½ inch plus, 3 inch angles plus a lot of other lengths of metal. I'm very impressed with the stock you have on that list".

"I just hope you have a workshop or shed" I said ruefully, *"where I can work".*

"Oh yes, we do have a shed that meets with your requirements"!

"Great Sergeant. Thanks very much! Can you show me please"?

"I'll do one better-show you and give you the keys so you can lose yourself in there! Have fun"!

The lock seems rusty I thought to myself. It took a while to open. On entering the shed I was pushing away cobwebs, God. The must and the damp were overpowering. I found the light switch and to my amazement the shed was completely empty except for a length of two inch hex bronze bar.

Macker

"Oh my God, I've got a problem".

I seemed to be about as useful as an ashtray on a Honda Fifty.

An empty shed. What to do next? Play for time. That's it.

I went back to the stores to complain about absence of materials. I got a *'scuchel'* from a (CRP) Kehoe.

"We have it and we don't, that's the way it is".

"What do you mean" I asked?

"Well we have it on paper"!

"So -what now"?

"You will have to order it from Clancy Barracks., in triplicate! The best would be three to six mounts before you got anything".

"Ok CPS sent it through"!

"Ah. As you are a private that may not be so easy. First we have to go through a

Macker

lieutenant, and then a captain then the C.O. and that could take six to eight weeks".

Going through the paces wasn't working. I was frustrated. So I decided to go straight to the C.O.

I was finally given permission to see him.

He sympathised with my plight but reiterated that Friday was the deadline.

"But sir where do I get the gear from"?

"Use your initiative -man"!

Outside the office door I stood a while to ponder. I was staring out at the top landing window into a back garden of sorts overgrown with grass. Right in front of me were two large metal frames. I ran down the stairs and into the garden. The frames were two basket ball stands just lying wasted. I got to work quickly. Collecting a few lads we carried one of the frames into my work place. I knew I would need the other one but there was not room for both.

Macker

I went to cutting the frame with my cutting torch. In a few hours the table frame was made, just to be sprayed and painted. The following morning it was finished and looked good.

I backed slowly away admiring my work.

"Whoops".

It was a Captain. I didn't recognise him.

"Oh that's a nice frame" he said putting his hand on it.

"It's still wet".

"Sorry about it Sir" I said and handed him a rag.

"It's a table frame Sir".

"Nice work private".

Later on I decided to go for the other frame but first we must get this one outside. I approached the Sergeant of the Day to ask for a few men to carry the other frame from the back garden. So with his help and five others we secured the second frame. I went ahead to get the cutting torch ready. When they dragged the frame into the shed I began to cut it up. Suddenly I could hear a lot of shouting and roaring.

"Stop it. Stop what you are doing, that's an order"!

I took my goggles off to see what all the noise was about. It was a Company Sergeant with an officer coming up fast behind him.

"What are you doing with our frame"?

"Your frame, CS"?

""Yes, my frame! Now who or what are you soldier"?

"Private McGowan-blacksmith welder CS".

Then another voice entered the fray. It was the officer who had been following the CS.

"What's up CS"?

It was the Captain who had admired the other frame and got his hand wet with paint. The CS explained what was going on.

Macker

"Well Sir I happened to look out the orderly room window and I saw a bunch of 'yahoos' robbing my basketball frame. I then followed them to where we are now Sir and this McGowan fellow was cutting it up".

"Right", said the officer pointing to me, *"turn that damn torch off. Now let's get to the bottom of this".*

Well with all the blame innuendos and blaspheming I was brought before the commanding officer and their four officers ACS and QM on Friday of that week with explicit orders to deny everything. Standing there the thought suddenly hit me that I could be shot for what I had done or worse. Well their Quarter master gave evidence of the ownership of the basketball stand or stands.

"It's a table tennis stand now and the other is in bits on his work flour"!

"So in conclusion Sir what about the destruction of our stands and what punishment will the instigator of this crime,

Macker

Private McGowan get" he said, pointing to me?

"Private McGowan will rebuild your basketball stands after I decide what to do with him. So Gentlemen please leave, I've got work to do".

The C.O. then turned to me and asked *"Have you anything to say for yourself, private McGowan"?*

"Well, yes Sir. You told me to use my initiative".

To my surprise he laughed out loud.

Chapter 10

Dead End Job

When we passed out as two Stars, we got every low down job the army could throw at us. One of those jobs was funeral detail and believe me there was an epidemic at the time. Those guys were dropping like flies...old IRA veterans and others. We had to be spick and span and polished up to the eye balls. Long nights were spent in bulling booths and whitening belts and shining brass.

Every funeral we were at, there was this old IRA guy who would complain and endlessly go on and on.

Macker

"You are doing it wrong - in our day we did it this way...."

No matter what way we did it he would be there to complain.

So this day we got a call out. Yes it's another funeral—here we go again. My complainant was sure to be there. We arrived at Glasnevin Cemetery early and we thought the funeral was under way. We hurried to the spot lined up by the grave where the draped coffin rested. We raised weapons and fired three volleys into the air as ordered.

We then found out it was the wrong funeral. Running to the other one we were in trouble. No blanks left and but there was *no 'Mr complainant'*. Delighted we went through with it and found to our amazement it was the complainant we were presiding over.

Macker

Chapter 11

Dooley's Bicycle

"Dooley! Get back on parade and in line you bloody lunatic".

"But Sarge...I've got to lock my bike. Someone tried to rob it the other day".

"O shut up and get back in line".

"Sergeant what was that man doing out of formation".

"Well Sir, you are new to our ranks and this man's name is Dooley".

Drawing the officer aside the sergeant explained.

"It's best to let it go sir. He has tendencies to imagine things and we ignore him".

"What sort of things"?

Macker

"Well... his bike Sir"

"What bike"?

"Well that's it Sir, he has an imaginary push bike".

"Does he now"? What have you done about it sergeant"?

"Everything the rule book allows, Sir".

"Handle it Sergeant-handle it".

"Leave it to me Sir".

Weeks went bye and Dooley cycled his imaginary bike to the parade ground to the annoyance of the new officer.

Then one day there was a surprise visit from a high ranking officer. On seeing Private Dooley near his car he asked for an explanation.

"Well sir, he was just parking his bike".

"What bike? I don't see any".

"It's imaginary Sir".

Macker

The sergeant explained that since his arrival in the barracks, Dooley had always arrived by bicycle.

"This is ridiculous"!

"Well sir he thinks he has a bike and we don't know what to do with him"!

"Get this 'madman' off my post and tell him to take his dam bike with him".

So the sergeant escorted Dooley to the gate with Dooley's walking papers. The Sergeant watched as Dooley parked his bike.

"Aren't you going to take your bike with you Dooley"?

"What bike? Sarge? Are you looking for your walking papers as well"?

Macker

Macker

Chapter 12

Feed My Sheep

The winter of '82 caught out the whole country. It was so bad that the army was called out to deal with the snow drifts. Headlines in most newspapers read *"Storm troopers take to the streets"* All kinds of tasks were given to us; from breaking the ice on the city footpaths to rescuing stranded motorists to delivering food and gas to remote places. By helping the others we seemed to forget our own.

In one case a certain Private Porter who was way out and up on Kilbride mountain side. His duty was to take care of army property. He was sent before the big freeze up on twenty four hour duty and waking up

Macker

the following morning was to his dismay snowed in. He managed to get a phone message through to his home base requesting food to last till relieved. When will that be he thought? With that the phone lines came down with the weight of the ice and communication was gone with headquarters. He did his best to preserve food and fuel.

Three and a half days passed and Porter became mighty hungry. Suddenly he heard a familiar noise comming closer and closer. Running out to the sound of helicopter blades he fell into snow drift after snow drift. He continued weaving his hands above his head, roaring and screaming at the *'chopper'.* Suddenly the helicopter towered over him and the doors opens. He sank down in the snow delighted that he had been spotted. His face fell as ten bales of hay dropped in front of him.

Macker

Chapter 13

Sailor Beware

I was detailed to the Curragh to pick up a couple of passengers on the way to Cove in County Cork. One was a young army man and the other a sailor. The young officer was to be dropped off at Longford. Well I reckon he was to start his first command. He was still wet behind the ears. The sailor boy looked bright. He was probably fourteen or fifteen years of age. He said he was attending the Technical School in the Curragh. We dumped the *"toffee nose"* and continued our journey. Looking out the windscreen of the vehicle we could see the Atlantic Ocean in front of us. Well aftercall we are an island nation and must need a navy even though we are the only navy who goes home to lunch on a push bike. So I got talking to the young fellow.

Macker

"Why the navy" I asked?

"Well I didn't pass my leaving cert and my dad ran amuck on me so I had to get out of there. So the navy was my way out".

"But you are so young looking.....how in the hell did you get into the navy"?

"They put me through a rigorous interview question after question. At the end of it all they told me I was accepted, due to my determination to succeed and my eagerness to learn a trade".

Then the youngster told me with a giggle the final question which they asked him.

What did they ask you"?

"Can you swim"?

"*Why*" I asked, "*don't you have any ships*"?

Macker

Chapter 14

Poor Old Nag

I was laughing to myself while doing the beats on duty. God knows you need a distraction on that duty. Suddenly a voice rang out. *"What's so funny private"?*

"Sorry Sarge, just a funny recall from the old television programmes...them black and white ones".

"Well why don't you share it with us private? After all you are renowned for your more humorous stories".

"Well Sarge the TV show was 'School around the Corner'. Paddy Crosby was the host. Do you remember Sarge"?

"Yes I do".

Macker

"Well there was this young boy on and poor old Paddy tried to get something out of him. Anything... a song, a dance, a joke or even a poem. The kid was a dud. It was like taking blood from a stone.

After much coaching the kid came through. He talked about something he remembered.

"Well Mr Crosby a nag fell down a "corpo" hole and broke its leg and the squeals of it Mr Crosby were unbearable. It was terrible sir. You could hear the old fellows saying - take it out of its misery. Then a man with a big gun came up and shot the poor nag".

"So" said "Mr Crosby they shot him in the hole!"

"Oh God no, Mr Crosby, they shot him in the head".

Macker

Chapter 15

At Face Value

Some people think that Monday morning blues belong to civilians only. Well you're wrong. Us in uniform get them as well. When the weekend is over and a week of same old same old starts again. Anyway, we are all around a table swapping spit.

"Hay Macker, you always have a yarn to toss about".

"What did you get up to on the weekend"?

"Ah! Well on Saturday I travelled to my 'grans' to help her out. You know a bit of painting, gardening and odds and ends. Well something strange happened on the way there. I was upstairs on the bus when the conductor arrived".

Macker

"Fares please! Fares please"!

"He bypassed the women in front of me. I didn't take much notice at the time but she was fumbling around in her bag. I paid the conductor my fare and then all hell broke loose".

"Thief Thief ", the women in front of me roared out loud and pointed towards me.

I looked around to see who the woman was screaming at. It soon dawned that it was me she was accusing. After I nearly swallowed my tongue I asked "What the hell is wrong with you woman"?

"You stole my purse"!

One of the lads at the table asked.

"How much did you get Macker"?

"Oh shut it" said another.

"Go on Macker, what happened next"?

"The bus conductor tore down the stairs".

"The bloody squealer" roared the men at the table.

Macker

"Hush, the lot of you, let Macker go on".

"And I hope you gave that so and so a bunch of fives".

"What happed next"?

"The bus came to a stop. The driver and the conductor came up the stairs".

"Before you say anything, I've done nothing wrong".

"In that case you will empty out your pockets" said the driver.

"I will not. I do have rights".

"The driver returned and drove off North and we were soon outside a garda station. Looking out the top window I could see a plainclothes and a garda heading for the bus. The driver must have radioed ahead".

"Jesus! Macker you were up the preverbal without a paddle" said one of my listeners.

"Hey let him continue the story. I'm dying to hear how he got himself out of that mess".

Macker

"Ok where was I? Oh yes! The plainclothes garda came up the stairs while the uniform stayed below, just in case I made a run for it. The police man stood in front of me looking me up and down. Then he started to introduce himself.

"I'm Detective Sergeant Hall" he said with his right handed extended as to shake.

"Ha!, Ha!, no way. I know that one Sarge".

"I see you know our ways".

"I don't Sarge but I'm no fool".

"Good on you Macker" said one of the lads, "there no flies on you and if there was they would be paying rent".

"At least may I know your first name" asked the Sergeant?

"Patrick"!

"Right Patrick, will you accompany me to the interview room in the station"?

Macker

"So everyone was interviewed separately and all the information related back to the sergeant".

"So! Ok Patrick can I see you alone in my office" asked the sergeant?

"Do I need council Sergeant"?

"O God no"!

"So we entered his office and the door was closed".

"Ok, Patrick the story is you're not guilty. We searched the lady's handbag and found nothing. So on instinct we phoned her husband.

"Ah! That stupid cow left it at home, was the answer".

"Sergeant. Why didn't you search me"?

"Would you have let me"?

"Without a 'breff' probably not".

"What now sergeant"?

Macker

"Well she is willing to compensate you rather then drag it to court. I suggest you take it".

"Not bad, five grand".

"Bloody hell Macker"!

"So I put my hand out to collect the check and the alarm clock woke me up".

"You fec.. b... Macker and they all went chasing me around the barracks with fists raised and shouting obscenities at me".

Macker

Chapter 16

Dublin Seanachai

"Summer Camp. It's that time of the year again. Where is it this year Sir"?

"Kerry if you must know Private McGowan. Kerry"

"Well that's a step in the right direction sir"!

"It beats Gormanstown hands down Macker".

The time passed fast and soon we were on our way to Tralee in County Kerry. All of the Corps of the Ordinance companies came to the summer camp from all over the country. It was Kerry's turn to host this year's one.

We settled in very quick and got to know the natives. Mostly on these camps we played sport against each other and would have good *'knees up'* afterwards. I was introduced to a few local lads who had heard of my exploits.

"So you're the famous scrounger and also a man of many talents".

"My reputation precedes me. Well if it didn't I would be late for all of my appointments".

"Hah! Hah", laughed a couple of them.

"Give us a Dublin yarn".

I obliged.

"When I was a knee high snotty nosed kid I would play with muck in the rain. One day a Kerry Garda approached me and asked me a question".

"What are you doing"?

"Making men out of muck Garda".

"Have you ever made a Kerry man"?

"Ah! Garda... this muck is not thick enough to make Kerrymen".

Macker

Chapter 17

Hungers Mother

Another day, another duty. This one was called *"Stand To"*. In other words we were ready and able to handle any emergency that came our way. We were a large number of men fully armed and on high alert for twenty four hours. Of course with a large gathering came hunger and greed. Imagine being stuck in a dorm type room for twenty four hours with a load of blokes.

Food became our companion. Well some guys took it to a different level, namely two or three. One was nicknamed *"Bugsie"* and the other *"Taz"* –short for Tasmanian Devil. Well late into the night Private Mangan woke me up with his finger to his mouth.

"Sheeesh! Sheeesh"!

Macker

With a low whisper he said, *"It's the Midnight Stalker"* and he pointed to the kitchen area.

It was a problem we were having with someone who was eating or robbing the raisins. We had named him the *"Midnight Stalker"*. So Mangan and I crept silently towards the cooking area and turning the corner we saw Taz with his two hands around this enormous sandwich composed of rashers, bangers, pudding, eggs and cheese.

"Good Lord, Taz", Mangan said, *"it's not a tapeworm you have it's a bleeden cobra"*.

Macker

Chapter 18

Trenches

We were out on a session on the weekend...the ones you never seem to get home from. Well we had a hard time of it down in the Glen of Imall in Wicklow. It never stopped raining all week and we were stuck in the trenches of our own making. It was one of our final tests before we got our third star. So while we were swopping spit and lowering the amber nectar, we were joined by one of the lad's grandfathers or great grandfathers. I can't remember but when he heard of our entrenched week in Wicklow he laughed out loud.

"You gorsoons are in the halfpenny place. I was in the trenches in the First World War".

Macker

"No joke"!

So he told us about a particular incident that had happened to him.

"It was a few hours before we went over the top. We got mail. Some got letters or homemade bread while others got woolen stockings. Paddy and I got a bottle of whiskey. To avoid it being confiscated by officers we drank it all. Of course in that war the reinforcements were in the rear. So the order came out. Pass up the reinforcements were going to advance. By the time word got to Paddy it was pass up the three and four pence we are going to a bloody dance".

Macker

Chapter 19

Duck the Bullets

Yes they nicknamed him Duck the Bullets O'Toole. Well that's the story this old codger was telling us one night in the mess. He of course was talking about World War 1. The trenches. Well of course we had all heard of *"All quiet on the Western Front"*. That's exactly what was happening. No one dare stick his head above the parapets for fear of Hun snipers. So Mick O'Toole, that's the guy telling the story, got a brainwave. He approached his commanding officer.

"Sir, begging your pardon Sir...what's a popular Hun's name"?

"Why do you want to know O'Toole"?

Macker

"It's a military secret sir".

"O K. There's a few names...Hans is a good one".

With that O'Toole dashed one hundred yards to his left and took up a position and roared across no man's land.

"Hans"

"Yah"

Bang.

One chalked up for O'Toole. This was going on all day. They counted fourteen Huns named Hans. The Huns copped on to what was going on. So they came up with a name knowing it was the Irish they were up against. So a roar came from the other side.

"Paddy you like drink"?

O'Toole kept his head down and roared back.

"Is that Fritsie?"

"No I'm Hans...why"?

Macker

Bang.

"That's a good officer we have lads. He gave me the other name that those Huns are called".

So came the name Duck the Bullets O'Toole".

Macker

Macker

Chapter 20

One Sergeant and His Dog

Sergeant O'Rourke was his name. A thicker man I never met. Well he had a problem. He had this mutt which looked something like a fox terrier. In other words... a mongrel.

Well he booked a week's holiday on the continent without thinking about the poor animal. Just before leaving he realized his error. What was he going to do with it? That evening he was in my work shop hoping that I would help him out.

"Look Macker, I can't bring the mutt with me to Spain and I asked the lads in my company would they look after it. And that

Macker

was a no no. So they let me down. Could you oblige me?"

Between me and you I think the lads were getting their own back on the sergeant for his former misdeeds. To them it was payback time.

"Sorry Sarge…no can do".

So in a joking manner I suggested he get seven labels and write Monday Tuesday Wednesday Thursday Friday and Saturday on them. Then stick a label on each bowl.

"This is brilliant Macker. Thanks a lot".

I had a quiet laugh to myself when he left. I forgot the whole thing until a week and a half later. The word was about that there was a certain sergeant boasting that he needed no one because he had come up with brainwave about his dog.

He left for Spain with a satisfactory grin on his face.

It was a different story when he came back. He was up before a judge to explain the

Macker

condition he left his dog in and what was the thinking behind it.

Macker

Macker

Chapter 21

Enemy at the Gate

I was in my workshop. My name was called.

"Hello. Are you in there"?

"Yes-I am".

"There is an officer to see you".

"All right-I'll be out in a minute"!

"Sir, what can I do you for, before you can do me Sir"?

"Ha, Ha, Ha"!

"I heard about you private and I hope your skills are as good as you are with your mouth. My name is Lieutenant Gorman and I've got a problem. I need a gate, eleven foot long and four and a half to five feet high".

Macker

"That's some gate Sir"!

"Yes-it is and I want it as soon as possible"!

"Well Sir, what is the purpose of this gate"?

"To keep the sheep off number three range in Kilbride"!

"How is that a problem, Sir"?

"They are being used as target practice by trigger happy recruits and I've been jobbed to stop it"!

"I see sir. I will write you a list of what I need. Private, this is from the top and everything you need, will be put at your disposal".

"Then Sir let's get started".

So we got the job done with gate supports and a wheel to wheel the gate to make it easy to open and close. I didn't erect the gate. I just made it. A few weeks later I was out in Kilbride on another job and saw the gate and the pillars I made. I laughed out loud. It had to be seen to be believed. What a laugh.

Macker

Sketch by Paddy McGowan

Macker

Macker

Chapter 22

Think Tank

Being a recruit wasn't all field work. There were theories as well...you know? Boring classroom stuff. Theories, like how far can bullets travel? How to duck, and all that crap from old sweat officers. But this day was looking good. It was a young officer and he looked in control of things. He then introduced himself.

"I'm Captain Duffy. I'm here to access your capabilities. Let me explain. War is not just bullets and bombs. It's about using your brain. Let me give you an example. If you haven't got the right tool–improvise".

So the good captain went around the classroom asking different questions of the lads.

Macker

"By God some of your ancestors were outrageous to say the least".

At last the captain came to me.

"Your name private..."?

So I gave him my name rank and serial number.

"Right then, private. Here's the scenario. The alarm is sounded. The barracks is under attack by a squadron of King Tiger tanks. How would you deal with this situation"?
"Now think carefully, private".

All eyes in the classroom were on me.

"Tiger tanks, King Tiger tanks, Sir"?

"Yes private".

"Well in that case Sir I would get my F-16' Jet fighters and blow them all to Hell".

"Where in the hell would you get F16's"?

"The same place you got your King Tiger tanks sir".

Macker

Chapter 23

Two Places At Once

The army loves to support sports among its ranks. And well we know this. Some of the most famous men were the show jumpers. There were others in the GAA, RFU, FAI and boxing, rifle and pistol shooting, shot putt athletics among others. The list is endless. Of course-every sport has its supporters-none greater than our Sergeant Bingham.

Soccer was his game and Manchester United the team of the demi gods. He worshipped them so much it was rumoured that he had a shrine built in the spare room with altar and all. Well the big day arrived. Manchester-United were to play Liverpool

Macker

but the good sarge was caught for regimental duty. Asking himself over and over what he would do, he went sick and got off the duty. The weekend passed and Monday came into it's own. A voice rang out.

"Sergeant Bingham the Company Officer wants to see you in his office as soon as possible".

Soon he was before the officer who did not seem at all pleased.

"Sergeant, I know you have a doctor's note to exempt you from your duty this past weekend but it didn't exempt you from your football. Did it"?

"What do you mean Sir"?

"Well Sergeant your picture is on the back of the Star newspaper".

The Company Officer showed him the paper.

"Whooah", said the sergeant "he made the Star the lucky git".

Macker

"What are you on about"?

"My twin brother, Sir".

"You don't have one" yelled the CO.

"I do now Sir".

Macker

Macker

Big Bang Theory

Chapter 24

It's this time of the year again when firemen and gardai go nuts. This particular year a consignment of dodgy fireworks were seized from a Chinese freighter down on the Dublin docks and like everything else the problem was passed on to us in the army. We had the enormous task of disposing of the said items. We were Explosive Ordinance Depot (E.O.D.). Unlucky for me I drew the short straw to drive the E.O.D. officer to the Kilbride rifle range on the day Ireland were to play England in a soccer match. So we arrived at our destination and started to unload the truck.

Macker

"Good God" said the officer *"how are we going to get through this lot and get back to the match in time for the kick off"?*

We found a ditch and started to dispose of the items one by one. This was the safe way but *'needs must prevail when the devil drives'.* Then suddenly I saw an old tar barrel.

"Sir, would this barrel be of any use"?

"At last you are using my brain, Private".

So we emptied what was left of the fireworks into the barrel and packed it down with stones. The officer then lit the fuse and we headed for a safe place.

"Hold your ears"!

There was a tremendous bang.

The noise was deafening. When the dust settled there was an enormous crater left.

"Wow" said the officer, *"we'll suffer for this tomorrow".*

"On to the match" I said.

Macker

The following morning I was summoned to head quarters where I met with the officer again. I knew this recent episode could backfire on us but to our surprise we received a thank you from the Chief Of Staff.

As it turned out we had solved two problems. First we had got rid of the fireworks and secondly the army used the crater to get rid of surplus waste they needed to dispose of for years.

Macker

Macker

Chapter 25

Did You Hear What Your Man Said

Like the Garda's *"Blue flu"*, the army had their protest. It was called *"Army Deafness"*. To find out how serious this threat was, the army conducted their own investigation. It started with a pilot scheme to take place in Saint Brican's Hospital on the North Circular Road in Dublin. Of course you always know the army ask for volunteers and of course you also know what that means.

"You, you and you. You just volunteered".

At this time our old friends the *"Gas Man"* with a sidekick called Porter were taking up temporary resident in the aforementioned

Macker

hospital. A store room was set aside for the pilot scheme. The original purpose was to store spare beds. So when empty it was a very narrow long corridor type room. Guess who was at the top of the queue-none other than the Gas Man and his side kick.

They tossed to see who would go in first with an understanding that what was said to one would be told to the other. Porter won the toss and entered the interview room.

"Please close the door behind you" was said by the interviewer in a very low voice.

So Porter did as he was told.

"Get out" said the interviewer *"there is nothing wrong with your hearing"*.

Porter left the room and whispered to the Gas Man.

"Whatever you do don't close the door".

The gas man entered and heard the voice telling him to close the door.

"Close it yourself you lazy git"!

Macker

Chapter 26

Tuppence For All

You would have to admire the gall and ingenuity of some people. I was in my workshop one morning when the *'Gas Man'* came in.

"Hi Macker. Could you give me two pence please? I'm short to make a phone call. Ye know... women. If you don't call they create an awful stinker".

I gave him the two pence and said,

"*Get off with yourself*".

So, he left but he had a grin on his face. The kind of grin you have when you get one over on someone. I didn't give it much thought then. Later that day I was in the mess

Macker

having a drink with Fred. He asked me a question.

"Did you see the 'Gas Man' Tyrrell today"?

"Yes as a matter of fact he dropped into my workshop earlier today. "Why".

"I don't know", said Fred *"–something I can't put right in my mind".*

"What do you mean"?

"Well I saw him in the orderly room earlier".

"Our orderly room"?

"Yes, and also in Tentage Storage Transport and our main storeroom".

With that a head pops over and into our conversation.

"Well it seems we all have the same problem" said a 2nd Battalion head.

"Hi Macker, didn't mean to butt in but the Gasman seems to be up to his old tricks again".

Macker

"What do you mean Porter" said the 2nd Battalion head?

"Well he's hit every one he could for tuppence".

"I don't understand Porter"?

"How many guys do you think is in this barracks? That's a hell of a lot of tuppences - isn't it"?

"Knowing you Porter - I reckon you're the one who could work that out but the gasman beat you to it first"

Macker

Macker

Chapter 27

By Special Delivery

We had a couple of days leave. So myself and Noonan went on the binge. We started in an early house in Tara Street. Noonan headed for the poolroom while I was getting the beer in. After getting the drinks I also headed for the poolroom.

"Hay Pa, you're not going to believe it".

"Believe what"?

"The bleeding barman is a 'rubberie', honest?

"Macker it's a bit early in the day to be pulling a fast one".

"Don't worry you'll soon find out".

Macker

"I will in a few minutes. I want to get this one down".

After a while Pa went out to order two pints.

Pa came back to the pool room with a bewildered look on his face.

"Macker you were right on the nail and don't that beat all".

"What Pa"?

"Here we are in an early house hoping to get that early start over everyone else and the blooming barman beat us to the draw".

The *'said'* barman approached the poolroom on drunken legs.

Of course the barman went one way and the drinks went the other way.... to the floor.

"Ooops" bellowed the barman.

"Oops" went us.

"What do we do now"?

Macker

Pa suggested we rest the poor fellow on one of the soft pews. Just as we were lifting him onto the seat the back door opened and the manager came in.

He took one look and copped on

"Are ye all right lads? I'm sorry about this. Any damage done"?

"Ah just two pints that went to the floor" said I, *"but get his nibs sorted out first".*

"Thanks lads you're a good sort. I'll fix you up with two pints on the house".

Pa suggested we leave as soon as possible and under his breath said *"bad luck to this place, you know what I mean. Imagine an early house that has the barman langers before opening hours".*

We drank up and left and headed into the city centre where we did a pub crawl for the rest of the morning. Come lunch time we got a burger and chips and started all over again. We drank some more. We ended up in Slattery's of Capel Street and had a few more pints there.

Macker

"Well", Pa said to me, *"we need to check our finances".*

So we put our money together and found we were going short. So Pa said to me that he would have to go and get a few bob somewhere.

"You hold the fort and I'll be back soon".

I looked out the window and saw Pa flagging down a taxi. What on earth is he doing I asked myself... He had the cabby drive around the block. As you know Capel Street is a one way system. The cabby came back on to Capel Street and parked outside a pawn shop. Pa pawned three rings and his watch. He got back into the taxi and they drove round to the main door of Slattery's. Then he paid the cabby and walked in head up high. He was proud as punch as he sat down.

"Barman set them up again and when that money is gone we will see what will happen next. Right Macker! So we are doing what we set out to do. Drink ourselves silly".

Macker

Time was moving on and the drink was going to our heads.

So the barman offered us a bowl of soup and rolls.

"It's OK lads, it's on the house".

We gave thanks and said *"it's was very thoughtful of you".*

"Well the way you lads are going, you need it".

We had our soup with rolls and they tasted good.

"Pa", I said *"we are in the driving seat".*

The boss man behind the bar just looked at us and laughed while shaking his head.

"You guys".

So we continued where we left off. Then that moment I dreaded came. We were low on funds again and Pa said to me.

"Any ideas, Macker"?

Macker

"Give me a moment to go to the jacks and I'll see".

When I came back, I said to Pa, *"what do you have left?*

His hands opened and he showed me a few punts and loose change.

I took the loose stuff.

"Just trust me".

I disappeared and came back with a smile. I sat down and ordered two. Pa had that bewildered look on him again.

"You ordered two"?

"Yep".

With that the front door opened, letting the sunlight in behind it. The silhouette of a young well dressed man in a tin of fruit (slang for suit) came over, handed me a brown envelope and said, *"Patrick it's what you ordered and may you have a nice day".*

"Thank you" I said and then he left.

Now Pa was really confused

Macker

"What just happened there" he asked?

"That's another story. Don't ask me now".

I took a few notes out of the envelope and put the rest in my back pocket.

"We're back in the driving seat".

We drank 'till closing time and still had plenty for of money for a taxi home.

Macker

Macker

Chapter 28

Heinze

Yes, you may well ask, what is a *'Heinze'*? Well it's not as much what it is as who it is. My first encounter was when we were celebrating in the Rathmines Inn. Those that were there heard an awful commotion outside the pub. The Gardai were running around like headless chickens. Then a Garda Sergeant tying to make sense of it all said,

"What on earth's going on"?

The young Garda told the Sergeant that the culprit or culprits have run down the laneway beside the Inn.

Macker

"Then don't stand around here looking dumb. Get after them or it".

We were bemused at what was going on. We watched the Garda run down the lane in pursuit of the unknown disturbence. There were four of them. Soon after that, the Gardai came running back, with their tails between their legs.

"Sergeant, we're not going to tackle that".

"That! What are you on about"?

"It's Heinze Sergeant".

Now my curiosity was aroused. Who or what was Heinze? In the meantime another garda car arrived. This one was a plain one. Dicks.

"Right Sergeant", said the Dick.

"What's up"?

"Heinze, Oh! God not him again. All right Sergeant where is he"?

"Down the lane. No, wait, here he is coming up".

Macker

It was then I got to see the Heinze.

"Good Lord"!

"It's Drago from Rocky Four".

The big Russian was built like a brick shit house. He was six foot five or six foot six at least in height and almost as wide. The lads I was with and myself were all ushered back into the inn. So, I asked Fred and the others who he was.

"You don't want to know. Why he nearly killed me and the others about a month ago".

For weeks I kept hearing about Heinzie's exploits. Man he was something else. One day I was jobbed in the gym where a boxing tournament was to take place. They army contenders would be coming from all over the country. My job was to make safe all metals pertaining to the rings and take down the basketball stands which were springs loaded into the roof trestles.

Any way one of the bouts was light heavyweight. Dublin verses Galway. I was

Macker

looking on when the Galway chap was shadowboxing in his corner. Then the ref called on the fighters to face off. On turning the Galway chap took one look at his opponent who turned out to be Heinze and then he melted into a jelly. One punch by Heinze determined the outcome of the bout. The poor Galway man hadn't a chance. But Heinze was getting into all kinds of trouble with the powers that be. So, he lost his place on the Olympic team at the start. But it's amazing what a woman can do. Yes like the song goes he was brought to his knees by a thing called love.

Macker

Chapter 29

Gift Horse

Christmas is the time of the year I hate the most. Everyone is begging for something or other. It's supposed to be JC's birthday and some of those Holy Joe's take down their bibles on Saturday and Sunday. Then they screw everyone from Monday to Friday. What a load of cobblers. Well this particular Christmas I was asked to make a special effort to attend our unit's Christmas doo.

So off with the overalls and on with the *'tin of fruit'*. That's slang for suit for those who live outside Dublin. That night I entered the dining hall to a round of applause and the odd bit of slagging from some of the lads.

"Hay Macker, I thought you would be wearing new overalls" came one of the jokes.

Macker

Another shouted,

"Jesus Macker you scrub up well"!

"Yes", I said *"this time I had a bath and put water in it".*

That got a laugh. My CO came over and shook my hand.

"Nice to see you Private McGowan- you do look well".

"Thank you sir".

Even the Pauline *"one"* said the same.

Then I ran into Paddy Noonan, my pal. He's the one, if you remember, went on a binge with me earlier in the year. I had never told him where I had got the money to keep paying for the drinks.

"Gee Macker you do dress down well. Nice one- free counter at Cleary's was it"?

"No" I said *"look at the inside label".*

"Jesus Macker, that's a Louis Copeland".

"Sheesh don't tell anyone".

Macker

"Where did you resurrect said garment"?

"Where else"?

Then the penny dropped.

"On that day, yes, you were handed an envelope by a well dressed geezer".

"Now you know. My brother works for the man".

Macker

Macker

Chapter 30

Big Stink

Being a recruit in the army restricts your movements as you can imagine. You can't go from A to B without a written pass. You have to have a leave the barracks pass, to leave the state pass, a weekend pass, and a laundry pass. Now there's a pass I could not understand. Well you see it's like this. The army caters for your every need, health, food, clothing, fitness, self defences, map reading and orientation. But they don't have a laundry; so we have to go to *"Civy Street"* to get our washing done; with a laundry pass of course.

There was this P.A (a military policeman) guarding the main gate. So we would have

Macker

to show our passes to him to get out. But this PA had it in for me. I don't know why but he would check my laundry bag or my weekend case every time I would leave the barracks. So I decided to fix him good.

I had a foot odour problem –a bad one. I saved up all my dirty socks and put them into a plastic bag. So the next time I went on a weekend pass I put my laundry in my rucksack and headed for the main gate. As usual he pulled me over.

"What's in that bag recruit"?

"Just laundry CPL"

I was ordered into the gate house.

"Bag on the table and leave the list".

"Step into the corner".

"Yes, CPl Lowe"

He opened the bag to a nose full that would have killed an elephant.

He never bothered me again.

Macker

Chapter 31

Pathfinder

I got a call one Monday morning. Defiantly not a good time for a call. The morning after the night before, if you get my drift?

"Macker, EOD wants you up the North".

"The North?"

"The North of w'ah"?

"The North of Ireland".

"Why me? They have their own people".

"They want you and your particular talents".

"What's up"?

"Ah that dam robot —something up with it".

"You're to take Willy the Wheel as the driver".

Macker

"Take two armed privates as escort".

"Oh! you're to pick up a spare wheel for the robot in Clancy on the way".

"Anything else, Sergeant"?

"Yes Macker. You're to check in when you get to Dundalk. Check with the Orderly Room. I think it's 'Bandit Country' you're heading for. Ha! Ha! Its helmets and flack jackets for you and the crew. Don't forget to check with Dundalk, that's the order of the day and from the very top".

"Understand Macker!"

"Yes Sergeant".

So we picked up the spare wheel and another passenger.

"No rank"?

"Deffo".

"Army" said Willy the Wheel.

If anyone knows Willy would. For God's sake I think he was there at the founding of the state. We started our journey for the

Macker

North without any small talk and made good time. We parked outside the Orderly Room. The non ranker got out and said thanks.

Willy asked, *"What's next Macker"?*

"Why your guess is as good as mine".

I reported in.

"Private McGowan, Sergeant".

"Ah we've been expecting you. You made good time on the way. But we have a problem".

"Now your destination is Forkhill in the heart of bandit country. But the beef is we have no pathfinder to lead you there".

Suddenly a voice rang out.

"Sergeant I can lead them there".

"You, Mulligan"?

"I didn't know you were from that part of the country"!

Macker

"I know it like the back of my hand Sergeant".

"I'll get them there".

"That's sorted. Private McGowan you will report to your officer Lieutenant Hesian on your arrival. He's the one that asked for you. I don't know why".

"That's what I said".

Soon we were on our way.

"We seem to be driving around in circles" I said to Willy.

"Yes it does Macker".

"Hay you!, 'pathfinder' where the hell are we"?

"Ok, wait till I get my bearings".

Suddenly we were facing down the barrels of British guns. Well I can tell you, Willy lost the head.

"You silly plonker, a 'Pathfinder' you are not. Look at the mess we're in 'you dozy f....r".

Macker

Willy then asked. *"Why are you here"?*

"I was trying to get away from guard duty".

But I was looking at the British officer.

"Hay Willy- guess what"?

Willy looked.

"Our passenger from earlier. He's the captain in this British lot".

"Something stinks here Macker" snarled Willy

"Good afternoon gentlemen. Ok! My lads only lower your weapons, they are on our side. They were kind enough to give me a lift from the republic. Thank you again".

"May I be so bold as to ask what is going on?

"Sorry, Patrick is it? If I tell you I would have to shoot you".

I laugh.

"Well would you be so good as the show us the way".

Macker

"That I will do gladly Patrick".

So he drew a little map. We thanked him and went on our way. We drove for about ten minutes. Then Willy slammed on the brakes. We were thrown all over the place.

"What wrong now, damn it" I said.

A land rover had come out of a concealed entrance blocking our way and another was behind us blocking out retreat. Poor Willy was losing it.

"Calm down Willy they are ours".

"Oh God look whose walking towards us. It's Hesian and he doesn't look happy to see us".

"Hello Sir, sorry we got caught up, back there".

It was then that I noticed that he had a coil of detonation wire already rolled out.

"Whoops sir we did not know".

He ignored me and went for Willy calling him everything under the sun. I eventually got my word in.

Macker

"I know sir it looks bad but we ran into British Intelligence posing as recon".

"Oh my god how bad can it get"?

"Please sir let me finish".

"Go ahead".

"We have done everything by the book, but that British recon unit did not give full disclosure of what was going down. And we nearly walked into an explosives 'no go' area".

"Sir I would add-never take an untested pathfinder into the same area. So please Sir, I think Willy should not be blamed and that Sir will be my report to my CO when we get back. Do what you will sir".

Macker

Macker

Chapter 32

Pathfinder 2

For three weeks after our foray into *"Bandit Country"* we were constantly questioned by MP's. Then came the Court of Enquiry.

"In your own words Private tell us what happened on that day"

"Before I do sirs, I would like to know who was that strange 'civy' who travelled with us from Clancy Barracks".

"Why would you like to know that" asked the Senior Trial Judge?

"Because Sir, it's him who should be standing here and that so called 'Pathfinder'

wherever he has got to and not the four of us".

"I'm sorry private I cannot divulge the identification of that man".

"Well Sirs, he's the British officer who intercepted us on that day, and sent us into the 'kill zone' and that Sirs is my evidence. If you want to keep it secret Sir's, I will go public".

"You will what"?

"With all due respect Sir's, I will".

"This court stands in recess while we deliberate".

They came back in after a shot interval.

"Well Private. I must ask you to sign on the bottom line of this paper. It's the Official Secrets Act. When you do that, we will let you know the answer to your question".

I did so and was handed a slip of white paper with the mystery guest name and rank and why he was here. They reckoned

Macker

he was spying and got caught. This was his way of getting even.

"So! Sir we are pawns in this game".

"We had to do this Private to make it look good. Sorry. You and the others are dismissed without charge".

Macker

Macker

Chapter 33

Wallpaper Party

I was stationed in Cathal Brugha Barracks in Rathmines in the Dublin suburbs. To me Rathmines is a city within a city. It's also known as flatland. Well at the time I was sharing a flat with three others. Two of them were army like myself and the other was a plumber. Of course we got on like a house on fire. Because of this we socialized together. Our local watering hole was Slattery's. It was a great pub. Late in the evening we would watch out for guys leaving with six packs and follow them. There would be a party on somewhere tonight. We have gate crashed nine or ten of those. The secret is there is always a *'Mick'*

Macker

or a '*Paddy*' who is attending and you bring your own. Well one night there was nothing doing. So we were about to leave when we were approached and invited to a wallpaper party. Yeh beware of Greeks bearing gifts and all that.

"No, No, on the level just bring your own".

So we headed for the address we were given.

"What's a wallpaper party" I asked as we walked through laneway after laneway?

"Search me" was the general consensus.

"Well here we are".

We knocked and were shown into a large near empty room but for a three legged table and two and a half chairs. A dozen people or so were gathered around a blazing fire in the heart. Music was supplied by a pocket radio.

"Pull up the floor and relax. Sip some beers".

Macker

"Hay when is the Ballyfermot Brass Band due" I asked?

Hours passed. The table seemed to disappear along with the half chair. So I called over our host.

"I would like an explanation please".

"OK" he said.

"Me, and my mate have been living in this flat for the best part of fifteen years. After all this time they are throwing us out. We took this flat as unfurnished. So now we are burning everything".

"So next to go is the wallpaper" I said.

"You catch on fast" said the host.

I'm telling you that was some party. Well I suppose they have other types of party like Tupperware, Avon, kiddie clothes and other types of parties. So wallpaper seemed to be a good idea. Oh yeah they even burnt the floorboards. So I heard.

Macker

Macker

Chapter 34

Arm of Truth

My brother Philip was also in the army. He joined about a year before me. Now if the truth be known he was a likable rogue and loved the easy life. I often wondered why he had joined the army in the first place. Anyway-halfway thought his training he broke his arm so he was let off with light work; like keeping the home fires burning and running erands etc. Coming to the end of his training we got an invitation to his passing out parade. Shortly before the appointed date I had a visitor at home where I was doing some work. It was Philip who walked in. I asked him how his arm was and he replied,

Macker

"All right"!

"By the way" I asked him, "what are you doing in your uniform"?

"I'm supposed to be in Saint Brican's Hospital getting my arm checked by X ray".

Suddenly he slipped off the plaster cast and sighed with great relief.

"Bloody thing is damm itchy!"

"Philip you're on the con".

"But of course Macker".

"Is your arm broke"?

"Really"?

"Of course not"!

"Where did you get the arm piece"?

"Mate of mine works making the plaster casts in Brican's Hospital. The rest I leave to your imagination. Some mate he turned out to be" said Philip.

"What do you mean" I asked?

Macker

"I had to buy my own white paint for the last six months".

"What about the passing out parade".

"I'll be there with the rest of them. But I won't be square bashing for no one".

"Ha! Ha"!

Macker

Macker

Chapter 35

Long Drop

The pavilion in the Phoenix Park was a long-standing sports ground for the army. Annual sporting games were contested by all four commands. Sadly, this is no more. Except for one day only, the football match of all four commands which would be held later in the year.

As usual volunteers were sent to work on the main building. Those who had the skills like roofers' plumbers and carpenters, and generas dog bodies of course. This was done on the cheap. No engineers. So us band of merry men were given our working orders from a *'Luie'* (that's a one 'pip' officer).

Macker

One of our group raised his hand.

"Sir".

"Oh, it's you CPS Mooney! Are you going to complain as usual"?

"Sir that roof does not look safe".

"I know CPO, that's why you are here and if you happen to fall and break your leg or your arm we'll mend them".

The *'Louie'* left and we got on with it. About a couple of hours later I noticed CPS Mooney still had his two feet firmly on the ground.

"What's the 'diddly doory' CPL, I asked"?

"Ah, it's you Macker. The very man. Give us a hand with those mats".

So we dragged the exercise maths to a chalk mark on the floor. Mooney started to arrange the maths to suit himself and kept looking up at a spot on the roof.

"That should do it".

"Do what" I asked?

Macker

He ignored my question.

"Now Macker! I want you to wipe away that chalk mark and leave this area pronto".

So I went back to where I was working on the toilets and a few minutes later I heard shouting. I ran towards the noise and looking up I saw CPL Mooney falling through the air shouting these words,

"Claim, Claim".

"Well I'll be a sucker" I said to myself.

Macker

Macker

Chapter 36

Big Shine

We had this officer who came late to our unit. Rumour had it that he was not very popular. He was also very witty in a cunning way and he himself was very particular in who he liked and disliked. He hated those above him and those who had a higher control in the *'non com'* camp of the army.

One day our CS Sergeant was looking for scalps to take, all because of his hangover or her indoors had kicked him out again. There were five of us lined up for a grilling. Suddenly there was a loud roar from an upstairs window. It was the new officer.

Macker

"CS (as they were known) on me now and double it".

"Now"!

"Hoh. Hoh," one of us said.

"Who's for it?

"He is", said one of our gang.

"I know that officer and he hates bullying tactics".

A short time later the CS was in the new officer's room.

"CS reporting- Sir".

"Right CS. I would like you to sit in my newly acquired chair".

CS did as he was ordered.

"Now slide to the left and then to the right. Now slide forward, now slide back. Now CS that will be all. Leave me".

"But Sir, why"?

Macker

"You may well ask? Because you are not a good judge of men and have no common sense. You are only fit to wipe the dust of my newly acquired chair. Good day CS".

Macker

Macker

Chapter 37

I Spy With My Little Eye

"Hi Macker! There's a new guy coming today. By the way be weary of him. How he got here beats me".

"Well Fred your word is normally good for me. There seems to be bad history between you two".

"You've copped it Macker. You don't miss much".

"Well Fred, you might as well give us the lowdown".

"OK, Macker. A couple of years ago there was only a few of us left in a competition for a most prestigious award. So it was up to us two to decide the winner. If we agreed we would sit an exam of twelve questions each. And of course this guy objected. It's not fair,

Macker

it's not fair. I've been at a disadvantage since this started. No one gets on with me".

"Just sit the exam. You got one and a half hours" said the officer in charge.

After we had finished we were both called to the office.

"Well we have the results. You both got eleven out of twelve each. But apprentice of the year goes to apprentice Travis".

"Hah...but sir, you said we got eleven out of twelve each".

"Yes, you both did. But Private Travis had, 'don't know on question two' and you on the other hand had 'don't know either'".

Macker

Chapter 38

That Damn Yank

"Tom and Fred were having trouble with the Yankee bloke. They were flat mates of mine. Anyway this yank was putting down the Irish army as a bunch of misfits. Not to be slandered by the yank they came up with a plan. It's a pity I was not there to witness it".

"So go on, what happened" asked one of the lads?

"Tom and Fred got this 'Duck the Bullets' warlord to stage an armed robbery on our flat. Well the warlord's hobby was making toy soldiers and painting them and collecting replicas of the more famous guns.

Macker

Anyway, the plan was simple. McTolbit the 'warlord' would enter the flat at gunpoint with a threatening manner. Tom and Fred would jump him and save the day. Thus proving that the Irish army were a proven force and not to be messed with. A party was arranged in the yanks flat. Well it was their turn anyway.

Like all plans we never made allowances for the unexpected. The yank's girlfriend was upstairs washing her wig when she saw McTolbit in black gear with balaclava on all flours creeping through the back garden. She then phones the guards and all hell broke loose. For weeks after there was a lot of explaining to do for Tom, Fred and especially McTolbit.

Macker

Chapter 39

Point Of Difference

Being a recruit, living close together with so many guys, you tend to learn a lot. For instance we had a *'mouthpiece'*. He did nothing but complain. It was always about one thing or another, especially about the fact that he was always being pulled up about his own high esteem. For instance, remarks about his general tidiness or about his locker and bed space were being bandied about. Always he felt everyone was talking behind his back. He was kinda paranoid and he had a right to be. Words were dropped like;

"The next time he has a shower let's hope he turns on the water",

Macker

or

"If his feet were amputated his ankles would still smell".

So one night he ran amuck. All hell broke loose. He threatened to jump out the window. Of course the Lewie and the Sergeant came on board.

"What the hell is going on here" asked the sergeant?

"Well Sarge, they were all slagging me behind my back".

"Like what recruit"?

"Like 'I'm not fit to live in a pigsty' for instance".

"Macker, Where are you. Is this you're doing"?

"Sarge, I had nothing to do with it... as a matter of fact I stood up for him".

"How do you mean"?

"Well, they all say he is not fit to live in a pigsty and of course I disagreed with them".

Macker

"You do, Macker"?

"Oh yes Sir, he is fit to live in a pigsty".

Macker

Macker

Chapter 40

Forehead

The tuck pulled up outside the clothing stores. A young private got out. *"I'm looking for Private Forehead".*

"I'm Forehead".

"You're Forehead? Hang on there", said the truck driver, *"I know you. You were in the platoon before me. Your name is Forrester, Forrester Forrest....that's it Forrest. Who put that name on you"?*

Just then I arrived and answered for Forrest.

"It's a long story".

"Well I've got a couple of hours to kill".

Macker

"It started about eight months ago when a certain private in this unit was up for theft and damages to army property. The said property was a couple of basketball stands".

"Yes I heard about that. How did that go down"?

"It went well for us. The private in question got off on technical grounds. But it didn't sit well with a certain Captain from the school of music. He's been trying to get payback. So every time our unit does a block duty the said Captain would volunteer himself for duty the same day. Anyway we come back to Mr. Forehead here. One of our tasks was a guard duty.... all day and night. The Captain would stick it to the crew. On one of those sneak attacks we got wind of it and our private Forest here was on the beat. So me, the guy behind the basketball incident, went out to warn Private Forrest to be on the alert. As usual Forrest was dozing. I was convinced that the good private was bitten by a tsetse fly and quiet capable of sleeping on a clothes line. With that I heard something and called out "halt. Who goes there"?

At the same time I pinched Forrest. Meanwhile I crept back into the duty room unnoticed.

"It's Captain Hayes".

Forrest called, "come forth and be recognized".

Forrest asked me to get the gate keys for the Captain which I duly did. While the Captain was passing through our friend here, Forrest muttered something under his breath."

"You sneak".

The Captain challenged Forrest but my quick thinking saved the day. "What he said Sir was that you are unique".

"Oh" said the Captain and began to sort out the roster. He then stopped short.

"Private McGowan. Who is that man on guard'?

Macker

"Forest Sir. Private Forrest".

"What did he mean when he said I was unique"

"Well Sir he said you are always uniqueing up on us sir".

"Then the whole guardroom erupted with laughter. So loud it brought the MP to check it out. The Captain went berserk and said,

"Forrest, you'r for it".

So the name stuck.

Macker

Chapter 41

Noah Meets Columbus

We were participating in a joint military operation at Baldonnell Airdrome. The units were from all over the place. Everything was going great until the last night when a few yanks began to get a bit loud and boastful.

"Ooh you Irish. You really are a Mickey Mouse outfit. Ha Ha. What a joke".

With Lesley and Travis there I knew it would not be long before there would be a response. About an hour later the two came from the rest room together. Then I knew it was about to start.

"Hay! Where are you from?" said Travis to one of the yanks.

Macker

"Idaho".

"Where on earth is that"?

"America".

"Where's that"?

"Never heard of it. Have you Lesley"?

"No! Have you ever heard of Columbus", said one of the yanks.

"Columbus" said Fred Travis?

"Is'ent that the guy who had that ship. A huge big ship-with all funny animals in it. Yea like the humpy backed camel and the long neck geese. Yea with all those animals doing their number two's, it got smelly. So Columbus and his crew shoveled all that shit overboard.

"No", Fred said.

"That was Noah who did all the shoveling. It was Columbus who discovered the big piece of shhitt".

Macker

Chapter 42

Who Done It

We were on a call out with the EOD (Explosives Ordinance Division) team. We were on the border a couple of miles from *'Bandit Country'*. When we arrived we saw a pub burnt out. Of course it was no ordinary pub. It was an IRA hot spot. According to the guards it was a bomb not a fire which destroyed the pub. Between the fire brigade and our team, we discovered the explosive device. With that "*Willy the Wheel*" muttered under his breath to Da Duffy and me.

"Do you get me lads? Are you seeing what I'm seeing"?

Of course we nodded together in agreement.

A Sergeant of the guard took an interest in our behavior and questioned our interest to the said property.

Macker

Willy started to stare at the guards and asked *"what is it with you Sergeant"*?

"You seem to have an interest in those things" said the guard suspiciously.

"I know who done it" said Willy as he raised his eyes to heavens with confidence.

"I also know how it was done".

"All right Sherlock lets in on it".

"Well it was McGuire and Patterson who were the main culprits".

"Never heard of them" said the Sergeant.

"Now as to how it was done... First you will observe there is no glass to be seen. So the pub was cleaned out before the fire, making it premeditated. As to the bomb..... Well it was the Calor Gas bottle put in the center of the fireplace. So Sergeant you can see it was a fire and a bomb. The abbreviation of these two words is a firebomb".

"Elementary, my dear William the Wheel" chorused Da Duffy and myself.

Macker

Chapter 43

News about News

It's true to say all branches of employment fraternize. It's also true to say they have a breakup drink at holiday periods and of course this extends to the armed forces. So one Christmas a group of us from Ordinance headed for the Concord Pub in Rathmines. We sat up at the back of the pub where there was more room. So in the late evening the manager came up to us and offered us soup and sambos. Just when we needed it. That really put a gleam in *"Willy the Wheel"s"* eye.

"Grub great".

I turned and said *"Good God, Willy you would eat the hind leg of the lamb of Jaysas"*

Macker

Then I ducked as he lashed out at me and we all had a good laugh about it. After a while I went to the bar for more soup and sambos. I was followed by *"Willy the wheel"*, *"Hungers Mother"* or wherever else he was called. We had our meal and looked at the telly.

Then came this barking loud noise running in our ears, over and over again.

"Press or Herald, Herald or Press"!

Suddenly Willy gets a hard rap across the back of the head with a rolled up newspaper.

Turning in anger he shouted *"What the hell"?*

Behind him was a twelve year old girl with a bundle of papers under her arm

"Want a newspaper mister"?

"No" said Willy. *"I get all the news from the television"*

"That may be so but you can't wipe your arse with it, can yea"?

Macker

Chapter 44

Hearsay

The trucks were parked, which left no room for some of us. So we got a travel warrant for the train from Cork.

There were eight of us in all; an army sky pilot; two sergeants; one corporal and the rest were privates including me. Knowing our luck the train was packed. We found ourselves in this carriage full of sporting women. We heard them say something about a mini marathon in Dublin. So we couldn't help overhearing a conversation between two of the girls.

"Ah go on- tell us" said one.

"Ah go on, Anne, tell us"?

Macker

"Well we agreed to meet on the beach. Dave and me. So Dave came straight to the point. I'll show you mine if you show me yours".

I said *"Whah!"*

"Ann, you asked to see his first".

"Yes so what"?

"Then he unzipped it. I was in disbelief and awe at the size of it. Then I asked with bewilderment.

"How are you going to get it up Dave"?

"With your help Anne we could get it up".

"How dare you talk of such filth, you shameless hussies" interrupted our sky pilot.

Ann and her friend turned to him.

"It's about kite flying you silly dirty little man. Never earwig".

Macker

Chapter 45

Some Cat

"Hi Tom".

"Hi Fred".

"Hay. What happened to the Main Gate and the barrier"?

"Some damn mindless truck driver forgot to brake and slammed right into it, taking the pillars, barrier and the gates with it".

Tom and Fred had a chuckle telling me.

"There you go Macker, a set of gates and a barrier to make... We know you are up to it."

"Right Macker?"

"Right".

Macker

Days passed and I got stuck into it.

One morning we were at our elevenses and *"Willy the Wheel"* made a comment under his breath.

"Yes Willie?"

"Well, is that you talking or just chewing a brick?"

"Well, what of it Macker? We are all sick of extra duty because of that damn gate".

"Don't blame me Willy. I didn't crash into it".

"When will it be finished?"

"When the builders get their fingers out".

"Oh talking about the gate..." I said,

"You know that pile of sand that's there?"

"Yes" said Willy?

"What about it?"

Macker

"Well you know that mangy cat that's always hanging about there. Well he done his dirties in the sand".

"So what"?

"Well what was so amazing was that he turned around and buried it".

"Ha! Ha! Cats always do that Macker".

"I don't know Willy..."?

"This was different somehow".

"*How*" asked Willy?

"This one had a shovel".

Macker

Macker

Chapter 46

Stamp of Approval

Being in the Ordinance we used to check all weapons no matter where. Not me of course. I'm just a welder but I used to accompany those on some of their inspections. One of those was in G.H.Q. (General headquarters) where we met the most boring private I've ever had the misfortune to meet. He seemed to be a mindless automaton and I was assigned to him. After a few hours of complete silence with him I broke the ice and asked him what his duties were.

"I'm a document and letter conversationalist".

"Wow, that's a mouthful. What does that entail"?

"Well every correspondence that has passed through here in the last hundred or two hundred years, I have catalogued".

Macker

"Interesting" I said.

"You must have signed the Official Secrets Act and got the stamp of approval".

"I like you" he said to me. *"My name is James Beehan. What's..."?*

"I'm McGowan but they call me Macker".

"I suppose they call you Bags".

"Yah".

"Well we all have our crosses to bear".

Well we talked a while and finished up his section.

"I'll see you around".

So when we completed our inspection of the unit we were invited to the mess for a few drinks where I met *"Bagsie's"* C.O.

He told me that Bags was weird.

"Kept to himself. Never mixed with anyone. I asked him once had he any ambition".

"Beach front property" was all he said.

Macker

"That's weird".

"Sir everyone has their own way" I said.

"Anyway", said the CO, *"I had a drink with Bags and that the last I saw of him".*

Years later I was in Spain and walked into an Irish bar. I had a drink and asked how much?

"On the house to you Macker".

I strained my eyes to see through the darkness of the bar. Then I saw my host.

"Good God! James Beehan what on earth"?

"Of all the bars and all the gin joints in the world you walk in to mine".

We both laughed hard and heartily.

"I'll join you" he said.

So after a drink or two he told me the story of all he had and how he got it.

"Well do you remember all those letters and documents I had to categorize? Well they

come in nice envelopes and what do those envelopes have"?

"Stamps".

"Persizelly, Macker. You sparked the thought in me".

"Whah..."?

"How did I do that?

"You must have signed the Official Secrets Act. Remember you said it when we first met. I started to collect the stamps and every two weeks I took a trip to the stamp fairs in England. I made a bundle. By the way, how long are you staying Macker?

"I'm flying out tomorrow".

"That's a pity Macker".

Well fair play to him. He has my stamp of approval.

Macker

Chapter 47

Things That Go Bump In The Night

I was awoken by my Sergeant.

"Hand of jocks and on socks".

"It's ours, Macker"!

"Pa O Toole"

"Oh. Wake Dexaroe. He's part of the group".

We called him Sergeant Dillon or Marshall and sometimes Bob Dillon. That's the kind of guy he was, a soldier one day and a poet the next.

So we went on our way. Half way through our patrol we came across a disturbance in bushes at the back of the Barrack Church which in turn was brought to the attention of the barrack C.O.

Macker

"Sergeant Dillon please tell this enquiry in your own words. What you caught this couple doing".

"I caught them humping sir".

"How dare you use such language in these hallowed halls? Inquiry dismissed until Sergeant Dillon presents his case in a proper manner".

So two days later the Sergeant was back.

"Well now Sergeant. Tell the enquiry what you saw".

"Sir on the night in question I pushed the hedging apart and saw that his pants were down and they were dangling. And her panties were down and her arse was bear. If that's not humping then I wasn't there".

Macker

Chapter 48

Ugg Lugg Maker

This particular guy tried to join the Irish Rangers only to be thrown out on his *'Derry Air'* with the words *"get that Ugg Lugg idiot out of here"* ringing in his ears.

"Sir", asked the Sergeant of the Rangers *"what's the story on him"?*

"Well Sergeant he was trying to join every known outfit in this man's army and I've got the lowdown on him from my brother in the navy. They took him in".

"Well the navy will take anything in - Ha-Ha, especially on those long journeys to the Med. Well anyway, on this particular trip, the journey was so boring that my brother the Captain called the Chief".

Macker

"Well, Chief we're here again-same ole same ole".

"Well Sir, there is an able-bodied seaman with us, a kind of oddball".

"Well what does he do"?

"Does he sing juggle dance or waltz"?

"None of them, Sir".

"Well what?"

"He's an Ugg Lugg maker".

"A what?"

"That's what he calls himself".

"Ok let's go for it. Anything to combat the boredom. Give him what he needs".

So *"Ugg Lugg"* himself puts in the list of equipment he needs, kitchen sink included. Day and night, he worked in secret with a clattering and banging that kept the crew awake at night. At last the day dawned and all hands were assembled on deck to see what had been made. On deck was this eight-foot-tall thing. The sheet was pulled.

Macker

There was sudden bewilderment on the faces of all who served.

My brother the captain was so shell-shocked he never recovered from it.

Well anyway he had enough cop on to give an order.

"Get that monstrosity off my ship".

They dragged and pulled the monstrosity to the edge of the ship. It was the most horrible ugliest thing you could imagine.

"Over with it" roared my brother the Captain.

And get this-when that monstrosity struck the water it went *"Ugg lugg, Ugg lugg, Ugg lugg"* as it sank beneath the waves.

Macker

Macker

Chapter 49

Boak....Boak Story

Nearly always in times of crisis the army would be called in. Bus, rail or ESB strikes were the normal. But this one was weird..? We were sent to County Cavan on a routine assignment. On arrival we found the townspeople were up in arms.

"Luie, drive on".

We arrived at the barracks and got settled in. Later we went for chow. *"How can you sit there when our town in a crisis"* complained one of the local soldiers"?

"Nothing to do with us, so we're told. Anyway, what's going on" I asked.

Macker

"There's a chicken strike…"

"Ha Ha," I roared.

"No, I don't mean that. There's a strike in the chicken factory and the workers have barricaded themselves in. This was going on for a week or two. Then the news came. The workers had left.… But they left the place in bits. Things got worse. A few days later thousands of chickens were causing a health hazard. The army was sent in to stave off a possible epidemic".

So a Sergeant was put in charge. Apparently he used to work there. So his recommendation was to kill all the chickens and freeze them. A daunting task considering the machinery for neck snapping of said birds was badly damaged.

"Right gentlemen, we will do this by the numbers. First we grab the bird by the scruff of the neck with the right hand; then we grab the birds head with the left hand; now by holding tight with the right the left hand will twist sharp to the right; then to the left; rendering the said subject

Macker

incapacitated; then throw over you left shoulder and start again".

So a few days later all that could be heard from the factory was, "*hane doo trea, hane doo trea*"... and, on and on. The story is that the Sergeant and his men outdone even the machine designed to do the job and the army saved the day again.

Macker

Macker

Chapter 50

Oh No Not You Again

Resting off from duty I went home to help out my Dad with the usual odd jobs around the house and the weekly shopping. When all this was done and put away we would go for a couple of pints. At that time my Dad's local was the *'Hogan Stand'*. Or was it the other one. I get mixed up between the two. Any way we got to the pub and it was black. You could not get your nose in the door.

"Aaah Dad, I think someone kicked the bucket. Where to now? Da, the Big Tree or the Red Parrot. Which one"?

"Naan, I don't like either on a Friday night. I think across the road- Gills".

Macker

"Dad are you mad? I thought you were barred from there".

"I doubt they would hold a grudge for that long".

"What do you think Pa.."?

"Well Da, once I don't have to wear a helmet going in. Anyway Da what happened? Why did they bar you..."?

"Can't remember".

So we went in. I ordered two pints and sat down. My first impression was that this was a real *local's* local. It was cozy and warm. Then I thought I could get used to this pub. What caught my eye next were the photos. They were all over the place. So I got up and had a good look around at the pictures.

"Whooh".

I was amazed.

Brendan Behan. He was all over the place with Gay Byrne, Ulick O' Connor and many more. After having a good look around I went back to my Da.

Macker

"Hay Da why are there photos of Brendan Behan all over the place"?

"Behan" said Da.

"Don't mention his name. It was because of him I got barred. Now I remember. The dirty up all night. Years ago I came in here after work for a couple. There was a load of celebs here. Like Noel Purcell, Danny Cummins, Gay Byrne and that guy McLiamoir and others. And here was this idiot with his shirt tail sticking out and drunk as a skunk. He was effin and blinding out of him. When I got the chance I made a complaint to the management about the loudmouthed idiot talking to the cream of society. Before I knew it I was out on my ass on the pavement and for a long time I didn't know why. So son, please do not bring him up again".

We never went back.

Printed in Great Britain
by Amazon